About the Author

Regina Wallmark is a businesswoman with experience from many perspectives. She has a master's degree in business with a major in leadership and finance. She has been a part-owner of a family business, has had her own business since October 2013, and worked as a consultant within finance for many years. She started her career at a bank, and continued within audit. She has learned that you need to take care of yourself and challenge yourself to be able to succeed as a business leader. To use daily strategies to become very efficient is a smart move.

Structure Is Key to Success

Regina Wallmark

Structure Is Key to Success

Olympia Publishers
London

www.olympiapublishers.com
OLYMPIA PAPERBACK EDITION

Copyright © Regina Wallmark 2023

The right of Regina Wallmark to be identified as author of this work has been asserted in accordance with sections 77 and 78 of the Copyright, Designs and Patents Act 1988.

All Rights Reserved

No reproduction, copy or transmission of this publication may be made without written permission.
No paragraph of this publication may be reproduced, copied or transmitted save with the written permission of the publisher, or in accordance with the provisions of the Copyright Act 1956 (as amended).

Any person who commits any unauthorized act in relation to this publication may be liable to criminal prosecution and civil claims for damage.

A CIP catalogue record for this title is available from the British Library.

ISBN: 978-1-80074-033-4

First Published in 2023

Olympia Publishers
Tallis House
2 Tallis Street
London
EC4Y 0AB

Printed in Great Britain

1
Getting Ready for Self-Mastery

To be successful in any area in life, you need to take care of yourself if you want to go anywhere.

And to stay successful in the long run, this is even more important. It doesn't have to be boring; you have to motivate yourself. How do you do that? This book will give you a set of tools to manage yourself, and to help you to remain strong through ever-changing times.

You deserve to be happy and loved. There is room for second chances in life. By the way, who is counting? People, perhaps even close ones, will let you down. But you can stay strong anyway. You will sacrifice a lot if you throw it all away – your dreams, what you are meant to be. Wouldn't it be really cruel if our dreams were just there to tease us and leave us feeling criticized? There must be a reason for us having these dreams of ours and planning for a future. If you didn't care about anything, you would end up as a robot, hoping that your feelings would disappear. But we're not robots; we are humans with dreams and emotions, and we can accomplish wonderful things.

Sometimes you, yourself, are the enemy when you tell yourself that dreams and hopes are childish or will never happen, that they are one in a million. Well, it will never happen if you stop trying. How do you get the motivation then to keep on trying? You have to sort out your own personal strategy.

You need leadership. You need to get in command, and in this book, you will learn how. It starts with you. It may hurt some when I say that, but we will go through this together in this book. In the end, you will say "I did it!" You will have transformed yourself into both your guardian angel and your best friend.

You need health. You can improve your health, and you need to start right now. Eating fruit before lunch each week will help you to transform your stomach to suit a healthy lifestyle. Are you overweight, and if so, do you know by how much? If you go to a doctor, you know what they will say. They will check your BMI (Body Mass Index). So, check that online, and take steps each week. You will get fifty percent more energy from not being overweight. It's your body that will hold you up and take you places, because a healthier body affects your mind and your mindset, and decreases depression.

A few more pieces of health advice so we can kick off and get started. Think of it this way: switch from French fries every day to French fries on Friday and Saturday evenings when you celebrate your weekly success. Later on, you will have taught your stomach to not appreciate French fries, and they will no longer have any hold on your appetite. You will have found so many other flavors you love. The same is true of sugar addiction. It will take you two weeks to get rid of the hunger for sugar. Start to do the same thing as with French fries. Switch from candy to healthier chocolate if you eat sugar each day. Learn to appreciate healthier things, and you will notice that everything will taste too sugary. You will start to appreciate other flavors and natural sweetness, instead of sugar and unnatural sweeteners. As for bread, eat whole grain bread instead of French fries, potatoes, rice or pasta as your evening meal on weekdays. Make your lunch your main and largest meal if you work afternoons, or dinner if you work physically in the evening.

To recap – eat fruits for breakfast and before lunch. That is sufficient to work on. Drink a lot of herbal tea and a whole lot of water every day. Have a steady lunch if you work in the afternoon, but no French fries during weekdays. Eat whole grain bread instead of French fries, potatoes, rice or pasta for your dinner. Make your portions smaller, and have only one regular portion, not any large ones. If you feel hungry, drink water. Hunger is a feeling you will master too.

To dig deeper into this, we need to understand that what we eat and drink and how we take care of ourselves have a huge impact on our life. Science says that our cells reproduce, so we are not the same person we were three years ago. That is quite amazing, and it really shows that it is very important that we take care of ourselves. Think about a child: it is easier to take care of a child if you have routines with exact hours for when to eat and sleep. It is worth the investment to have a good routine with a child as fast as possible. A child sleeps better if they are not hungry, and eats better if they aren't tired. A routine with a good night's sleep will create an appetite for food and vice versa. The same with us grown-ups and young people.

It is commonly known that sleep is something we need to recharge and let go of feelings of worry. Drink some chamomile tea two hours before sleep, and you will feel relaxed. Have no screen time one hour before bedtime, and no television in the bedroom. Sleep seven to eight hours daily. Some say nine hours. See what you need, and take thirty minutes of meditation if you feel stressed during the day. During the meditation, sit down outside, if possible, in a park, and look at the beauty of our nature around us.

Feel the wind, and look at the trees and flowers. Or meditate indoors by a window, looking out on a park or some water. Think about small things in life. In fact, it is not a small thing to be alive. That is a miracle. Find things that you are happy about, things in life that you are appreciative of. Find these thoughts, sit by yourself for thirty minutes, and let your thoughts go into that mode of appreciation. Think about at least five things you are grateful for. The meditation has the purpose of getting you in the mood of appreciating things you are happy about, and it will reduce your stress. Take a deep breath when you start, and take a deep breath when you are done after thirty minutes. Stretch your arms and back a bit when you stand up again.

This is a good thing to do every day.

Make your time management schedule. Divide the day into four boxes with six hours each in them.

Just to view your time in these four boxes is a good idea. Draw four boxes on a piece of paper, and first make a review of your day so far. Write into the boxes what you have been doing today and for how many hours. Write in the boxes how many hours you slept the night before. Review your day so far. No need to blame yourself, just write it all down so you can see it. That's the first step.

Step 1: Write in each box what you have done today.

Step 2: Organize the four boxes into different topics.

Step 3: Make an overview, and calculate how much time you spent on things that were not necessary. The goal here is to find where and what you can take time from.

Step 4: Make room in one of the boxes for time you want to put down on your dream every day. Take time from something else, and overwrite with a line what you want to take time from.

Step 5: Review your new time schedule and decide to make this your new schedule for the upcoming weeks. Adjust it to suit your life and circumstances.

It is good before a new week to make a review about your week and what you have achieved. Do you need to adjust your time schedule, or can you improve it even more to make more time for your goals? Set up smaller goals along the way, and create a plan for how to reach your goals.

Save it on your computer desktop, and write out the plan so you can see it and visualize it several times every day. Let your plan with your goals be an important part of your everyday life. Have your plan on your phone too.

Pep talk to yourself is the next thing you need to do. In this area it also starts with how you view yourself, and what you say about and to yourself. To build up your self-respect, you need to say good things to yourself, and in that way convince yourself that you are capable of reaching your goals. This is an unconscious message to yourself. Try this and see.

Before bedtime, when you brush your teeth, look at yourself kindly in the mirror. Compliment yourself on the good things you have done today. Do this in the morning as well; look at yourself kindly and say, "I will do good things today." During the day it is good to compliment yourself for good things you have done, even small things. If something bad happens, say to yourself, "I will learn from this, talk about this later, and do good things from now on." This will encourage you and give you chances to improve your day. Even small things and small steps in the right direction are important progress toward a high **self-esteem.**

Analyze your feelings at the end of the day after dinner. Don't analyze when you are hungry is good advice. After you have de-stressed from the day, analyze the feelings you have had during the day. Sort them out in a document with good feelings and bad feelings. Try to see a pattern. Ask yourself, "Why did I feel this way? Why did I react this way to both the good and bad feelings?"

Get to know your reactions, and manage your feelings this way. When you try a new diet, you might feel hungry, so drink more water and herbal tea to feel alert, and not hungry, sad or angry. Eat more fruit if you are hungry.

Ask the following questions:
1. When I reacted positively or negatively, was I hungry or had I just eaten something?
2. Can I connect my reaction to something in particular? Why did I get this feeling that ruined my day or made it better. Look for conclusions.
3. What did I do well today that made me feel more joyous and happier, and that gave me energy?
4. What do I need to avoid to not lose my focus in my everyday life?
5. Sort out areas that you identify as problematic, and look for alternative ways to handle these circumstances. Can you view them as important lessons for self-control, or look upon them as challenges that will improve your patience?
6. Write down "two sides of the story" conclusions. What if I choose to look upon this from another angle?
7. Learn from your reactions and feelings, and encourage yourself to master your feelings better next time when something difficult to master occurs.
8. Encourage yourself for your good feelings and achievements today. Write down your wins for the week, and celebrate in small portions the upcoming Friday or Saturday, together with your family or friends that really care about you and your progress.
9. Write down your areas of improvement and organize them into a to-do list and a wish list of improvements. Think about where you need to start or easily can start, taking it one thing at a time. Prioritize in order of importance.

Use this analysis as a tool for improvement to get

insight into yourself. Make these moments of reflection into something calm and cozy with a cup of relaxing herbal tea. To learn to become better is something very beautiful. Good job to you!

2
Deal With Your Emotions

When you use the nine questions on the previous pages, you will gain more insight about yourself and your mood swings. Good habits will keep your mood and temper more in balance, and this will help you a lot.

Don't be too hasty with decision making, for instance; consider if the timing is right for the decision, and if it is necessary to give an answer right away. Say, "Let me think about this for a couple of hours, and I will get back to you."

Give yourself time to make decisions when you are in a relaxed mood, so that you can consider the options thoroughly. Don't say "No" or "Yes" too hastily based on a bad mood or an impulse if you are hungry or tired. Make decisions according to your plan, so you don't end up on someone else's path or plan instead of your own.

Your emotions are your emotions. How can you more fully control your emotions? If you start to use the previously-mentioned good habits for your health, you, and others, will notice an improvement in your mood and attitude. When you go into a supermarket, being hungry will create different outcomes. The stores know that, the bakeries in the store are proof of that. We react to what smells and looks good, and we buy more when we are hungry, right?

Deal with those emotions which are tied to other

people's comments or attitudes.

When you are in balance, you don't react so much to what other people say. You probably recognize that. You wonder why you reacted a certain way to someone else's behavior. It has to do with your mood and what balance you are in. Good habits help you to be more balanced and not overreact so easily.

If someone says something provocative to you, wait a few seconds. If you know them, just look at them. Otherwise, just walk away. If you know the person, listen, and wait a few seconds before you respond. This way, you will give the other person the chance to reflect upon what they just said or did.

If you feel yourself getting upset, angry, or sad, take a deep breath, and say that you need a moment, and want to take a break and talk about it later. Decide on a time that suits you, and walk away. This way, you will get your feelings in order, and get the space to sort out your emotions and the message you just heard and are about to respond to. Take a few deep breaths and decide what you will say. Answer calmly and in short sentences that you agree or disagree and why. Don't get into an argument, just confirm that you heard what the other person said and then say what you think about it. You are entitled to your opinions and feelings, and the other person is too. A disagreement is not a bad thing. It is good to get things out on the table so to speak, but do it when both of you are in the right mood. Don't start a war. No-one wins in a war. If the other person is hostile toward you, say calmly that you do not accept that behavior and just walk away.

This way you will show both yourself and the other

person respect even in a disagreement, and very importantly, you will teach the other person how he or she shall treat you. By treating people with respect, you will gain respect. No-one can demand respect; you get respect when you treat others with respect. And when you feel that you are in control of your emotions, you will gain a lot of self-respect. This will boost you with energy to continue on this path of mastering your emotions.

You also treat others with respect when you listen, and pause for a few seconds as if you are digesting their words. You can repeat what they just said to confirm it. Say, "Did I understand it right that you said…" and say exactly what they said. This way, you will give the other person a chance to correct what they just said and give them a second chance. You can then answer, and say your interpretation of it to give them another chance and see how they respond. A dialogue is important. Don't make a discussion into a monologue. When you listen and take into consideration what another person has to complain about, then you really show respect, and you will gain respect.

Everyone wants respect, but it is required that self-respect is there to really think you are worthy of it. So, to treat yourself kindly is very important. Forgive yourself, and make improvements every day, because you can't fool yourself. Make the needed steps to improve, compliment yourself, share the small celebrations with your family and friends, and you will love yourself and others. Self-love is needed to love others, and you are worthy of love in your life. Never forget that.

Give yourself a new beginning, another chance at a life where you grow into making good habits your everyday routine, and it will give your life so much love. Perhaps you thought that was not possible, but it is. When you are in balance, it is a result of having good habits and good loving people close to you. We are social beings, and need to have family and friends close to us online and in real life. There are many possibilities to keep in close contact nowadays with people you care about and love.

3
Start Building a Structure

My morning routine is one and a half hours long. The first thing I do is to make chamomile tea, about a quarter of a gallon, to drink while I make myself ready for the day, with one large spoon of honey in it when it is not too warm. I drink it slowly, and I don't eat anything at home in the morning.

I do morning meditation to calm down with my tea for fifteen minutes. I read a chapter from the Bible each morning. I do a morning workout with dumbbells and some of my favorite music, so I get the right tempo and movement to get my pulse going up, and so I feel very energized. I also do sit-ups and some other moves, and I dance in the living room to the music in the morning. Then it's time to take a shower. I open the window, and have the sheets wide open in the bedroom to cool the bed down and let in fresh air. Then I make the bed, and put the dirty laundry where it belongs, tidy and nice. I also take care of my flowers in the morning as a routine to give myself joy and make me feel grateful for life. I take out the trash so there is a fresh smell when I come home again, and I keep my home tidy and clean.

This hour and a half morning routine gives me energy and I look forward to a new day. At work I drink green tea and eat fruits and vegetables for breakfast.

As mentioned in the previous chapter about **Time management**, it is a good idea to plan your week. Ask yourself if you need to adjust your time schedule, or if you can improve it even more to make more time for your goals. Set up smaller goals along the way, and create a plan how to reach your goals.

Prioritization is very important, and for that you need a planner to have your map toward your goals in your everyday life. With good planning, you will have time for spontaneous things too. A good thing is to have both a to-do list and a wish list, so that you will get an overview of what is important to prioritize. The wish list can be used as a reward list for when you have achieved goals according to your plan. It is a very good thing to write down what you have done, so that you see at the end of the week how productive you have been. Celebrate your progress and your work with something from the wish list.

Block time out in the daily planner for your routines and even leave time for spontaneous things. Of course, you can switch times if something comes up, but get back to the plan afterwards. You will notice how much you will have achieved, and you will feel less stressed, because you will feel and see that you are very structured.

At work I have **a daily planner on my desktop**, and I also have it saved on my cloud. Have your plan on your phone too. This way, I don't have to have in mind what I will do, and don't get worried that I might forget something.

Depending on your job, you can do the same. Or, you can do this with things you need to do in your personal life. **Use your phone with alerts** so you don't have to worry about forgetting things. Write down on a piece of paper or in a file on your computer what you have done. Save it and put a date there. Save one document for each week.

To do list **Wish list**

A new week will have things that did not get done from last week, and new things you need to do. And those routine things you need to do every day should really be there too, even if you won't forget them, because you will see all the things you have accomplished during the week. That is very good, as you see how productive you are.

What you have put down on paper or on a document on your computer will relieve the worry, and will give space in your brain for you to come up with new ideas that might improve your work or your everyday life in some way. Create space for creativity. It brings so much joy and fulfilment when you suddenly come up with a great idea that you can try.

To be focused is an important subject to prioritize. Distractions are very common in our everyday life and it is important that we have a strategy for what we give our attention to. You can choose what notifications you have on your phone, and even choose VIPs, so you see their calls and emails quickly. Emails are important. Just read the subject line of the email, and delete and unsubscribe to emails that are not of importance. But that takes time. So, block some time in your calendar if you have a messy inbox that need to be sorted out and deleted.

Create different email accounts, and sort out to whom you give out these email addresses. **Build a structure** here. Have one for invoices for instance, or for finance. This is good to do privately too, so that you have a clear and quick overview of your emails. Reply only to the important ones, and then focus on your agenda for the day, what you have planned to do, and stick to the plan. Avoid distractions that don't have anything to do with your plan or your goals.

Distractions can be like someone throwing balls at us. If we try to catch all of them we will fail and lose it all. Therefore, you need to learn the skill of looking at and identifying what you need to focus on, and ignoring those other things which are only time thieves and distractions. This way, you will be in charge of your day, and will focus on decisions that are of importance. Use the **to do list and the wish list** to remind yourself to focus and to not get distracted.

Decision-making is also a skill that you can be taught to be very good at. When you have your plan and your goals clear in your mind, you can easily analyze a question or suggestion together with your plan and see if it is a good match or not. **If you are unsure, wait with the decision.** The risk is that you keep it on your mind anyway. Therefore, it is a good idea to block a time to make the decision that same day. Then, you can focus again on what you were doing. If it doesn't match your plan and your goals, say "No." You have to defend your plan and your goals by refusing irrelevant distractions.

You will **develop the skill of faster decision-making** if you write down pros and cons of the different options. Don't make it too complex; have a one-page maximum. If it is a large decision, you need to take a break. Perhaps think about it over lunch and take a walk outside before you decide.

To *not* take a decision is also a decision. I like that statement. You need to act, you know? Compare the options to your plan and see if it will help you along your path or not. Then it is easier to make the decision.

Make a few questions about the decision before you make it. Ask yourself if the decision will help you to reach your short term or long term goals more easily, or distract you from reaching your short term or long term goals. Ask if it will give you more time to focus on what you are good at, or if it is a time thief that will steal your focus and make your journey longer. Ask if it will make you happier and give you energy, or if it will steal energy from you. Guard your time and energy!

The decisions we make randomly are based on our previous experiences, and the interpretations that we have made. We automatically sort things as important or unimportant based on our previous experiences. But we know that this does not mean that we make the right decisions. We know that if we eat a lot of fast food, never exercise, and only sit in front of a computer or a television, we will gain weight, and the consequences of being overweight will sneak up on us.

Therefore, we need to **make decision-making something crucial** in our life. We need to be focused and make a fair and realistic review to make a good decision. Use the list above to review all the decisions in life, and you will see how much you will change your life for the better. Then, you can create new healthier routines in your everyday life, both in private and in your career.

If your way to deal with decisions is the arrow, you have to realize that the different situations or circumstances where you will make your decision have to fit in. Your arrow has to fit into the different boxes, so to speak. And you will see that there are areas that you will miss out on, things that you haven't taken into consideration with your decision.

Even if it is a similar decision to one you have made before, the circumstances have changed, so it is not an identical decision. Everything changes, and we need to acknowledge this in our decision making. A good decision last year might be a bad decision today. In uncertain times, business as usual might need to adjust to new circumstances. Therefore, it is crucial to develop the skill of decision-making. Use our questions previously mentioned and make a one-pager of pros and cons.

The good thing about good routines is that you will not have to make all these small decisions every day, because you have your daily planner and know what to do. Decision-making takes time and energy, so it is a wise thing to create routines and stick to them. Of course, if you see that your routines don't work, you need to adjust them. It doesn't mean that it is a bad decision if your routines don't work. Adjust and design your everyday life.

In decision-making you also have to take into consideration the effect it will have on others, both close ones and other people in general. We have a social responsibility, and that grows with power and influence in my opinion. It also has to do with how you will view yourself. And it has to do with how others will view you. More about our social life will be in the next chapter.

4
Family, Friends and Relationships

Everyone wants respect, and we need to feel loved and appreciated for who we are. In the first chapter, I went through the topic of self-esteem, how to deal with emotions, and how to pep talk yourself.

The word self-esteem says it all. You can build up good self-esteem. It starts with you. If you create good habits, like the ones mentioned in this book, you will feel more relaxed and in harmony, and you will cultivate solid self-esteem. You need good self-esteem to better interact with other people around you, both close ones and at work and other social events. So good healthy routines are a foundation for balanced self-esteem.

You can't fool yourself. Deep down inside, you will judge yourself unworthy if you don't live according to your values. Artists often get the advice from more experienced peers to be true to themselves, no matter what. That is very good advice, because it has to do with looking in the mirror every day. Good deeds give us the approval of ourselves and give us a good night's sleep as well. It is all tied together; you can't fool yourself about doing things that you don't approve of deep down. This is very important. Take care of your conscience; it is a gate-keeper for good and bad. Treasure it and build that guidance within your life.

Being generous is an important part of self-respect

because you show yourself that you are a loving person that cares for other people. It is better to give than to receive, as the classic saying goes. It gives you joy when you give other people your time and your feelings and other gifts or donations.

The definition of a gift means that nothing is expected in return. This is so important. You give to other people because you care about them, and want to show them that you love them. This is the definition of being generous, and you will feel a very good feeling deep inside. It will make you happy.

Good things that you do are a form of confirmation to yourself that you matter, and they contribute to life in the most important way there is. This is how you build a high self-esteem. You care about other people, and understand that they are an important part of your life. True humility is to see yourself in the bigger picture, and to see that we interact with other people in our lives.

Expectations in life are often a cause for problems. We have expectations of other people, in particular within our family and at work. Other people have expectations of us as well. Expectations that are not accomplished often lead to disappointments, and can lead to arguments and hostility.

An expression that is very interesting is the importance of **sharing the same reality**. A good thing to do in a family is for everyone to write down a wish list with ten things they think are important and expect from other people.

Then, you can compare the lists, see what you have in common and negotiate on what is important. Here you will see the need for balance; you can't demand that you get your whole list through and accept nothing from the other ones. This is very good for teenagers. You raise the perspective of mutual expectations and motivate others to contribute within the family. This can be done at work as well. Remember to keep a good tone and a dialogue open; no-one likes monologues.

The idea of **toxic people** has become very common in the last few years. What is a toxic person? A problem that has been raised is that many people who are called toxic will level this same accusation at others. What do we make of this?

To start with, the first pages of this book took up the subject of being responsible for our own feelings. We can interpret situations depending on our current wellbeing, and we can react differently to the same situation depending on how we feel. Counting to ten is good advice. That way, we don't tell people off in an aggressive manner, because then we could be accused of being toxic.

Everyone has a responsibility toward how we treat other people. Much of this comes back to our self-esteem Our self-esteem sets the limits upon how we treat ourselves and other people. Everyone knows the idea that we need to love ourselves to love others. This is so important. Our self-esteem will help us not to feel threatened by the success of others, and will prevent us from being jealous or feeling envy or that we can't control our life.

I stumbled over the expression **"Living in Integrity,"** and it kind of sums up everything. I will explain how. If we have cultivated self-respect, we respect others, because we understand that it is important for our wellbeing, and therefore important for other people's wellbeing.

That means that **if anyone treats us with hostility** or threatens us, we understand that we need to get ourselves out of that situation without wasting any words or feelings. Just walk away. If you have to say something, because it is within the family or within a company, say that you need a break, and that you do not accept hostile behavior toward you. Talk in a calm voice and walk away. Say that you will listen when the other person has calmed down. When you walk away, you also set the standard for yourself not to tell people off in a harsh way. You will gain respect from others, gain self-respect, and keep your energy for more important things. You will also keep hostility out of your life.

Science says that wherever there is a group of people, there are rules which get either the group's approval or disapproval, and sanctions exist as consequences. That is the culture that people create together. And when someone new enters a group the dynamic of the group is immediately questioned. Some cope with this well, and others don't because they feel threatened by what this new person will mean to the group. It is about what influence the new person will have on the group.

There is a moral code of conduct. It is important to understand and to set up rules of behavior both within the family and at work. Behavior that is expected gets approval in the form of support, and behavior that is not accepted gets disapproval in the form of sanctions. A sanction can be non-verbal, such as the silent treatment.

The silent treatment is a sort of sanction that is not accepted within the family or at any company. To live together under silent treatment or to be a victim of this at work is harassment and degrading treatment of others. If you don't want to associate with someone then don't; that is a completely different thing. Within a family or between colleagues who work together, this is not acceptable. The silent treatment is as bad as verbal aggressive outbursts toward another person.

Sometimes adults play the role of a victim like a game to get their opinions, wishes, and feelings taken into consideration. Almost like a child that lies on the floor and kicks and screams at the supermarket to get what they want, they make a scene. In dealing with a child, one tactic is to ignore it, or to tell them that they are making a fool out of themselves or threaten to do the same, and ask how that would look. Another idea with a child is to say before going to visits or to a store that they have to behave, and that if they behave well, they will get a reward, like an ice cream.

This works with adults as well. If you are polite and nice to my parents, I will be polite and nice to yours. That is an easy sentence to use with issues of sharing your time between your parents and your spouse's parents and relatives. Negotiating with the same set of rules is always key and quite easy to communicate. We all expect some sort of justice and equal behavior toward each other.

5
Stress

When we get stressed, our communication gets faster and we sound tougher and more aggressive. It is difficult to concentrate, and we make hasty decisions or might miss out on important details. Our heart beats faster and our blood pressure rises. We get less focused and our productivity decreases as a result. Even our relationship with others gets affected; it is easier to end up in conflicts with others when stressed.

To work under a heavy workload for a long time, like several months, decreases our productivity if we fall into some kind of **machine mode**. We are humans and not machines. Longer periods of time under stress or high pressure influences our health, and can even cause a heart attack.

There are some important areas in life that work as an antidote to the bad effects of stress in our life. A healthy lifestyle and a social life with family and friends is very important, and works as a recovery from stress. Studies have shown that people who have a strong social circle around them tend to manage stressful times better than those who don't.

Meaningful conversations with family and friends are so important. Of course, it is the same thing at work as well. Coffee breaks are a good time to have meaningful discussions with colleagues. Smart management at work allows for social settings where everyone has the chance to say their opinion and get respected for it too.

Taking into consideration the opinions of others by listening to them is very smart management by company leaders, because it fosters an open culture where spontaneous ideas will flourish to the advantage of everyone. The company listens and gets suggestions of improvements from engaged employees, while employees feel respected and feel that they make a difference and make more valuable contributions in their work.

The same holds true for family and with friends. The expression that we have two ears and one mouth says a lot. When we listen, we learn a lot about the feelings of others and their perspectives in life. This is an important way to show respect, to really listen and try to understand. This way we ourselves will gain respect because we most likely will get the same treatment back. We get listened to and feel that our opinion matters. We learn a lot from listening to others' opinions and points of view, especially from other generations than our own.

5.1
Anxiety

Anxiety can be a result of stress or a reaction to a crisis in life. Anxiety is a way for the body to say that you need to slow down and make time for recovery. The body gets into a kind of "energy-saving mode." It is important that you listen to your body and get enough sleep. Go back to the first chapter about sleep if necessary. Really focus on how to get a good sleeping routine, because this is when our body resets and sorts out impressions in our brain, and when we relax our whole body. Eight to nine hours of sleep are best, not more, because we need time to recharge and we do that when we work our body. We generate energy when our body works. This is especially important if we sit by a computer all day and don't move so much at work. We need to exercise daily.

Fresh air and exercise at a high tempo, preferably to some up-tempo music, will help you to cope with anxiety. The adrenaline from the exercise will reduce the anxiety and you will feel refreshed and happier. Therefore, it is a very good idea to exercise as a morning routine because it will start your day with both energy and joy.

When you have anxiety, it is quite common to get the feeling that you prefer to be alone, and there is a risk that you will isolate yourself. Plan for time with family and friends, even if this is only for a short while to start with.

See this as an important treatment to get you strong again, because you need to socialize. We are social beings and talking and listening to family and friends will help us to recover and get strong again.

5.2
Detox Your Life

Detox your life from bad habits, bad associations and bad influences. This is so important. What we feed our brain with, what we listen to and look at gets into our mind and affects our mood and feelings. This is no exaggeration.

We know that bad associations influence our feelings and our behavior. Toxic people have a negative effect on other people's health, and one person can destroy a culture at a workplace. One person can create a lot of problems within a home. Therefore, it is very important to solve problems and not ignore them, because they don't disappear. It will be more harmful if problems rule your life. Solve the problems that can be solved and make room in your life for joy and happiness.

What we fill our minds with is so important. It is even said that we can choose what we think about. Daily activities of **positive thinking** will give us energy and help us to appreciate life and become happier. Destructive behavior and destructive thoughts deprive us of happiness and harmony in life. Positive thinking gets us the right results; we get strengthened, become happier, and even our self-esteem is put back into balance.

Therefore, to look at destructive behavior within our families or tv shows or online is not a good thing. Soldiers often get trained by violent video games. That kind of says it all, doesn't it? We have to be careful about what we feed our brain with, as much as we have to be cautious about what we eat.

We are responsible for our actions, because thoughts come before our action and decisions. Our thoughts control our feelings, so we are responsible for our feelings too. We can learn to control our thoughts and think positive and uplifting thoughts, which encourages others around us. That way, we spread positivity around us that influences others in a positive way, like waves on water.

This shows how important our mood is when we make decisions, decisions that influence both our own and other people's daily lives. To be and to act in harmony is a strength that is developed through good habits and daily routines. It is therefore crucial that you keep toxic people away from you and your close ones, because they will tear down harmony, trust, and happiness.

You can't change toxic people; they will take away your energy and joy in life. It is up to each person to take responsibility for our thoughts, our feelings, and our actions. We can't change other people, so choose carefully who you have close to you and at your workplace.

6
Being Optimistic

To be pessimistic in life is like walking around in heavy boots made of lead. Try to swim in them and you will drown. Being optimistic doesn't mean being easily fooled or naive.

Being optimistic means taking into consideration that events can happen by coincidence and not out of planned evil or by conspiracy. Being negative can be a road that is hard to get out of. It might lead you to make completely wrong decisions, because you only base your decisions on negativity, and not on facts. To be optimistic is to be easier-minded, so to speak; you are not weighed down with troublesome thoughts which can burden you. Dark clouds hanging over us and blinding our sight with negative thoughts deprive us of energy and make us give up on life itself.

Being optimistic is not about being superficial and having a fake "be happy, be happy, be happy" irritating grin all over your face. Optimism is a feeling of harmony where you give situations, people and yourself a chance, and don't condemn everything into negativity.

Sad or bad days can be endured with an optimistic thought that tomorrow will be a better day, even if today was a heavy day. A belief in a better tomorrow gives you strength and comfort; you give life a chance to show you its beauty. Appreciating small things in life is truly a comfort in tough times. And there will be better days. There will be. In traumatic times, you need to rest. Like when you have anxiety, your body and your mind are slowing down the pace to help you survive and deal with hardship. A loss of a loved one takes time to live through, but you can learn to live with grief. In time, you will remember them. It is beautiful to honor someone's memory, to do things that remind you of them in a very beautiful way.

Being optimistic also means being able to forgive and forget and to move on. Sometimes it is easy and sometimes it is not. Write down your feelings and really try do understand why you feel a certain way. To think, analyze, and meditate on your feelings is also comforting for you. You must really think things through; don't just skip your feelings. See the positive side of a situation and other people, and give them another chance with a safe amount of trust.

Don't blindly trust anyone or everyone; that is naive. To be realistic is a good thing. To be optimistic is to see the beauty in life. To only see the worst in everyone and to see no tomorrow is to be very negative. Learn from your past. Put your experience into new situations, but take into consideration that circumstances might be different and might result in a completely different outcome. Never stop learning. Being optimistic is a choice and a personality trait that can be developed. Stay optimistic, not with an irritating grin that is.

Surround yourself with people who believe in you, who cheer you on and who want the best for you. Of course, you need to do the same for them.

Being optimistic even has an important effect on our health and gives us a life with friends in it too. Optimism is contagious, and very powerful, so spread joy and optimism wherever you go.

Being optimistic doesn't mean that you don't care about problems in life; it means that you are prepared for problems. You see them as something that is meant to be solved, improving your skills along the way. You don't sit down paralyzed and bitter and blame everyone else. It means that you make the best of every situation you are in.

Staying optimistic means that even in hostile situations you can see that there is a way out, so focus on that. Stay optimistic even when you meet negative people. Don't let them steal your peace and harmony away from you.

Appreciate the small things, the details, in life. Each day is a good chance to choose one thing that you decide to be grateful for. Write down things you are grateful for and take turns with the things you love and make them that day's grateful statement. "Today I am grateful for …" and fill in the blanks.

You know negative thoughts will only drag you down into unhappiness.

There is a saying that we choose what we think about. Try to capture the negative thoughts and write them down, and also write down the feelings they bring. Write down the flip side of that negative thought, and see if you can see the situation from another point of view.

Being optimistic gives you energy and joy in life, and others will say that you glow with happiness. And you will, because you think optimistic thoughts, and are grateful for even small things in life. You will have more energy to do things you love. Being optimistic is the best investment or gift you can give yourself and your loved ones close to you.

7
Motivation

Challenging yourself is an idea that I use regularly. Challenging myself helps me to stay competitive toward myself, to excel, and to become even more skilled at what I do. Challenging myself also helps me with new goals I set up. It kind of gets me in the mood to really give it a go.

Motivation can be very different from one person to another. Therefore, you must analyze yourself what has motivated you in the past, both in small things and bigger assignments. It is about getting to know yourself more, what you react to and what you do not. It is your responsibility to motivate yourself. If other people easily make you discouraged, then it is a good thing to plan when to motivate yourself so that no-one gets the power to disrupt and discourage you.

When you have identified things that make you discouraged, you can recognize those situations and physically take yourself out of them. We have gone through this before. When you are hungry or tired it is difficult to focus and you get upset more easily. Therefore, good routines with food, sleep and daily exercise are needed to prepare and boost you, by giving you the best circumstances you can influence and decide upon.

Planning your week is also a good way to see where you can block time to do what you need to do to motivate yourself. If there is something daunting you have to do, block time out to prepare yourself. Visualize both the worst and the best-case scenario. Make a list again with what you can do to influence the good scenario or best outcome and identify what steps you need to take to reach that best outcome.

Small steps toward the right decision are so powerful because you will, both unconsciously and consciously, reward yourself with approval. You will gain strength because you are doing the right thing and doing what you can to move in the right direction. When you use the routine to look yourself in the mirror and compliment yourself for trying, you will feel strengthened as if you are not alone in this. Smile kindly toward yourself with approval and compassion, and you will believe that you have what it takes to do this.

Rewards are also a good thing to motivate yourself. We do this when we train dogs, right? We are sometimes quite the same. Just as we say with children, "You have to eat the dinner first, then you can have the desert," or "You have to clean your room and put the dirty laundry where it belongs, then you can play that game." It is how we should reason with ourselves. It is common sense and our subconscious knows that so we cannot fool ourselves.

When you set up goals for yourself, also set deadlines and rewards. Don't forget your family and friends. Share your success with them and invite them or go to them with a cake or something to celebrate the success that you have reached. Ask them if they have any goals in life they want to achieve and encourage them to do the same as you are doing, but remember they have to do their part. So don't take over their project, so to speak.

If you have trouble with finishing a larger project, try to plan them in smaller pieces. Map them out in a plan and put events for celebration into the plan.

Visualize the part-time goals and the long-term goal by looking at the plan. The plan should have the end goal either in pictures or painted, so that you see it in front of you regularly. Checklists are also very good if there are a lot of detailed steps that need to be done. A checklist shows you that you are moving toward the goal and you will see how much work you have put in along the way. This will help you to not give up, because then you will see the large amount of time, energy and other resources you would be throwing away.

7.1
Plan Your Projects

Before you start a project, it is a good idea to write down different situations or outcomes that you have taken into consideration. This is good because when or if you get to a point where you feel like giving up, or question yourself or the project, you can go back to the initial discussion about the project and remind yourself of how the decision making was done before it started.

If there are circumstances that you have not taken into consideration, take a pause and readjust the plan if needed. Make a new analysis, identify any other possible outcomes due to the new circumstances and see what is needed. Here again, it is important to find a balance between the time, energy and other resources that have been put down on the project and what is left to be done.

If you measure the amount of time you invest in not getting things done, by wasting time on being uncertain or postponing decisions, you will see how much time you waste on nothing. Using the time management schedule is a good thing from this perspective, because it will motivate you to use your precious time on more important things in life, such as your goals and your close ones, dear friends included. The time ingredient in motivation is a good perspective to get you going so you don't waste time.

Another important motivation factor for you is

visualizing your goals and what you need to do to reach them. The goals or dreams we have in life are what we are meant to be, I truly believe that. Sometimes you need to kind of kick your own butt to get started and just do it.

8
Mastering Good Habits

Good habits help you to see things more clearly and not to be affected by emotion or impulsiveness.

I have already let you in on many of my good habits I use every day, but here is an overview. These good habits help me to deliver to the best of my ability and to have the energy I need. Go back to the first chapters in this book to get a more in-depth explanation of each. Here is a reminder:

1. Sleep
2. Time management
3. Food
4. Living in Integrity
5. Family, Friends and Relationships
6. Anxiety
7. Prioritization
8. Focus
9. Motivation
10. Generosity
11. Optimism
12. Expectations
13. Detoxing your life
14. Challenging yourself daily

If you **sleep** enough each night, going to bed quite early and sleeping your eight hours, you will learn this skill and get enough rest for your activities the next day.

Time Management is so crucial, including your eight hours of sleep. You will keep track of what you really put your time into. Time is your most valuable asset.

Food: Teach your body what you can eat, what gives you energy, and when to eat. It is good not to eat anything after seven p.m. for an adult. Your body needs a chance to digest what you have already eaten during the day. Herbal tea is very good to drink if you feel hungry. Late-evening snacks or sandwiches only lead you to put on weight.

Living in Integrity is so important; it's about how you treat and view yourself and that in turn affects how you treat other people, especially your close ones.

Family, Friends and Relationships are so important. It is said that you are like the five closest people that you interact with. You must teach other people how they should treat you. Mutual respect is so important. The only way to be respected is to show respect.

Anxiety is very common in today's uncertain times. Exercising daily is very good, because the adrenaline takes the anxiety away. Take walks outside with a close friend or loved one. Make the walks faster so you get your heart pumping and your lungs the exercise they need. Chamomile tea is very good for calming you down. When I had a lot of anxiety, I drank as many as seven large cups of chamomile tea each day. It was my cure, not chemical medicine.

Prioritization is also so key. Write down your to-do list and check what has been done, and what you can wait and do when you are not feeling as stressed. Get to know yourself and what helps you, either doing large things first and then the small parts, or the other way around.

Focus is of course important, and if you keep track of all of these good habits you will become very focused. A good schedule is a very good idea; check what you have done already, and have your calendar up to date so you know what to do next. You will not have to worry about forgetting things. You don't have to keep things in your mind, because you have them in your calendar and in your goal planner.

Motivation: You have to learn how to motivate yourself. Look at past challenges; what encouraged and motivated you in the past? Look at your goals, both the ones along the way and the long-term goals as well. Get the whole picture and understand the importance of doing the things along the way. Motivate yourself by setting up some time for celebrating your wins and your goals, and do it together with your family and friends.

Generosity gives so much joy in life. It truly makes you happier to give than to receive. As adults we have to remind ourselves about this now and then. It can be small things, gestures, or listening to other people, especially our loved ones. Larger gestures are of course very nice too, but making good gestures everyday will make you really happy and raise your self-respect.

Being **optimistic** is the best gift you can give yourself and your closest ones, and it gives you a lot of energy. Negativity takes away your energy and destroys many other good habits.

Expectations are good to keep in mind, both your own and those of others. It is often a cause for disappointment when expectations are not met. It is often a cause of conflicts too, so the way to avoid and solve conflicts is to know and account for everyone's expectations.

Detoxing your life is about taking responsibility for yourself and your loved ones. Again, we get so influenced by people we interact with, so we have to guard ourselves and our wellbeing. Be careful about the kind of energy you expose yourself to.

Challenging yourself daily gives you both joy and energy. It really gets you going and reminds you that you need that competitive mindset toward yourself to really give your best effort every day. It is what we do each day that adds up and creates our future.

9
Some Classical Leadership Styles

Cheering people on toward goals and a larger vision requires skill and a lot of strengths. When I studied leadership as a major subject in my master's degree almost twenty years ago, I decided not to adopt a masculine leadership style. "What kind of equality is that?" I reasoned, and I still do.

I have seen so many women during my career on the leadership ladder, and many have made the mistake of thinking leadership is a masculine trait. To be in charge is to be responsible, and if you view leadership as being responsible for other human beings, you kind of get back on your two feet.

I will go through some traits that have traditionally been common in leadership.

Autocratic leadership means that one person controls all the decisions and takes very little input from other group members. **Autocratic leaders** make choices or decisions based on their own beliefs, and do not involve others for their suggestions, advice or for a second opinion. Decisions where no-one else's thoughts are taken into consideration lose the advantage of the group's different individual skills; that is the whole point of having a group of people. It is important to remember that to listen, take input and then make a decision not in line with that input is not a form of autocratic leadership.

I have been working as a record label director and a manager within the music industry since 2015, and I have noticed that young people believe that the company makes democratic decisions. That is not the case. I was the investor, and therefore I had a lot of say. Since I was new in the industry I listened, but I was not in the position to be told what to do based on other's pressure, raised voices, or complaints. I might have been viewed as having an autocratic leadership style, but I don't. Deadlines require a decision and not everyone will agree with every decision one hundred percent. That's a fact.

For the past seven years, I have lived in Stockholm, our capital city in Sweden, and combined working in the music industry full-time with some short-term assignments as a consultant in finance and leadership. At one large company, I made a suggestion.

The CEO said in reply, "I agree with you, but you know we have to get everyone else onboard to agree first." I was shocked. I hope this CEO came to the realization that it is an illusion to believe everyone will like a change. Getting people involved in change takes a lot of hard work into the change.

Do not ask people, "Should we make the change or not?" It is important to get started and move forward with the change.

Make a plan together with the management team. Then, explain why the plan is needed to the coworkers, present the plan to them, and listen to input for a maximum of a few weeks. Take the input into consideration. If possible, listen to some representatives from the coworkers so they really get heard. Discuss why and how, and then execute.

It is important that decision-making does not have any prestige around it. Then it is more difficult to get people onboard, so to speak. A company with many employees of different experience levels will usually contain lots of different perspectives on the company and the direction it should be going in.

To be stuck in the good old days is not good for change. It is important to really listen to those who have a lot of experience, because they might say, "Well, we have already tried that and it did not work." It is a good thing for people who are resistant toward change to be able to clear the air with their thoughts and opinions and to come with suggestions. Often, there is a lot of worry about things, such as if people will get laid off. People react very differently to uncertainty.

The CEO at the large Swedish company I mentioned can be viewed as having a **strategic leadership** style. That refers to a manager's potential to express a **strategic** vision for the organization, or a part of the organization, and to motivate and persuade others to acquire that vision. This can be very time-consuming and expensive for a company that really needs to change.

Laissez-faire leadership is a strategy that historically has been viewed as a weaker leadership style. In recent years, it has been renamed **delegative leadership**, and it can have its advantages. But to leave the decision-making to others can result in problems where compromises turn things upside-down and decisions are changed.

When designing your leadership style, you can write down pros and cons about each of these leadership styles.

Knowledge about these leadership styles will help you in different situations, because you can remind yourself how the different traditional leadership styles would handle the situation.

Douglas McGregor's idea of "Theory X" and "Theory Y" is classic, and very interesting and useful when you design your leadership style. A business leader with a Theory X leadership style views people as lazy, only wanting their pay check, unable to motivate themselves and having no interest whatsoever in their job. A Theory Y business leader is the opposite and views people as seeking job fulfilment, wanting to be involved and motivating themselves. Something that I found out recently is that nowadays workplaces have a mixture of ages in their personnel, sometimes with cultural differences. Millennials, born in the 80s, and younger people have different expectations of work than older employees. Millennials tend to expect a Theory Y leadership style. They view their time and effort as important and want it to be meaningful.

A Theory X leadership style is often expected from personnel older than millennials. They think that the boss is the one who should come up with suggestions, directions and do not want to interfere with that. Some even think that if the business leader is not a Theory X leader, then there will be no leadership. Masculine personal traits are also viewed as leadership traits because they are used to them. I have worked within male-dominated workplaces my whole career, where ninety percent of the business leaders were men. And of the women who were business leaders, 99.9 percent had masculine personality traits.

Within international companies the leadership style is, of course, influenced by culture. In my music company, I worked for three years with a Chinese company. Before we started to work together, I paid for something called Business Sweden. Based in Shanghai, Business Sweden helps Swedish companies abroad and has offices around the world. I wanted to know how it was to be a businesswoman from another country doing business in China.

The report was very interesting. In China, there is a strong hierarchy, but it is not based on what gender you belong to. So, if you are a Record Label Director, like I am, being a woman doesn't matter. When I went there, I felt more respected than I did in Sweden as a businesswoman with a feminine leadership style.

10
Decades with Business Leaders

Thanks to my background within auditing, I have met many entrepreneurs, and they all have one thing in common: they love to talk about their everyday business. It is very interesting to listen and to see their excitement when they talk about their different business ideas.

Small business owners put in a lot of effort and hard work together with their families; it is a way of living. The motivation is often to build something and to make a difference in their everyday lives. One thing they have in common is wanting the freedom to choose what to do and what to focus on compared to be an employee. The responsibility can be viewed as a downside if you feel that you don't have things in order and under control.

This is similar to a position as an employed manager; you manage things and therefore have a greater responsibility. It gives you the space to influence and create to some extent. The ability to influence is a motivation factor to keep employees that you really want to stay with your company. Some do not want to have their own company, so a fulfilling job is their highest wish.

Solving problems or situations for customers is often another key ingredient to the feeling of job fulfillment. So, be sure to share that joy within your company. We truly all need good news. Achievements are important to share within the company to cheer everyone along with their good work. Business leaders love to talk about their achievements, so encourage others to share their achievements within your company, from small things to great things.

The freedom, creativity and influence are the drive for managers and business owners. We can implement this into a more modern kind of workplace. Success or achievements at work are a way to measure what is really working well within the company.

If some areas are not working or show no progress, there you need to dig deeper and identify what the problem is, or if there's no point in providing these products or services within the company. Time is precious, and this is often something that entrepreneurs are not good at. They easily get carried away with each new idea, or never give up on a bad idea. Here, a team with different skills is needed to really provide the facts on what is working and what is not worth putting time and energy into.

11
Design Your Leadership Style

To design your leadership style, think back on leaders that you have worked with, their dos and don'ts, and other people that influenced you in your life in bits and pieces. Write down some traits and situations that you have appreciated and some that you have disliked, and why. From here, you can mark words that repeat themselves. You will find a guide of words to use as pillars of your leadership style. Save it in a folder of leadership and fill it in with more insights and situations along the way. This way, you will have an updated leadership style that grows with your experience in life, and so will you. This will give you a more dynamic view of leadership.

I like the Myers-Briggs model of sixteen different personality types. I recommend that you use this model when you put together a team. The model is very good for solving conflicts as well, as you can talk to individuals and explain the problem so that they understand. I will not go in-depth into this model, but, as I said, I recommend it. But be sure not to judge anyone after these definitions. You may have made a miscalculation about them, and people change and develop as well. It is a good tool to understand differences and different behavior.

To divide individuals into introverts and extroverts is very interesting and not only done by the Myers-Briggs test.

The problem today is that a lot is required of the same person. You can, and of course the whole point of a team is, to have a diverse mix of different skills so that the team has many strong skills as a whole. But in recent years, much is required of a person. Often the traits required in your job description are the opposite of what you have.

Something that I tell artists is that it is a good idea to step into your role when you get on stage. You can flip a switch and become the person you have designed or a character you have picked. That way, you can remember who to be on stage to deliver a good show.

The same thing is true of your leadership style. You must design it. First, you need to develop and get a wider self-insight. This is very important. Your feelings and experiences are there so that you have compassion and understanding for other people, and so you can say no to behavior that is not okay.

I have worked at short-term assignments within finance, and at some companies they had paintings with words for the right behavior at work. At one company the paintings were the first thing you saw when you came to the office in the morning. There were more paintings with these words of conduct by the coffee machine as well. This is not that uncommon, but here it was a few words that everybody understood. This was a reminder for everyone at work and it really worked. I felt very welcomed and included in the company by my colleagues and the other words were implemented into the culture and shown by the workers.

At other companies I have seen a whole essay of the values of the company. That is not a good idea, since people don't have the time or interest to read it. It is much better to choose a few words and, if necessary, to give a short explanation of what it means and perhaps what it doesn't mean as guidance. But never use too many words. The point is that people will see it and not have to read it. The point is more to be scanned by the personnel at a glance at it. It is meant to be a picture of values that they take into consideration in their daily work.

Expect behavior that is accepted and this will remove behavior that is not accepted. This is so important. You create the culture as a business leader, and you have to pick the words for the values that are to be present at the company. People do as you do, so you have to be the role model. If you don't take on this role, someone else will.

Employees expect leadership at work, and you have to be in these shoes and guide the way. The values are the accepted guide to the behavior and strategies that will be used to reach the company's goals and vision. Unacceptable behavior will be out of the question if you set up clear values and explain what the values mean when they are implemented.

The famous model by Douglas McGregor about the leadership style Theory X and Theory Y is very interesting, and is quite easy to remember and use. As explained earlier, different people will expect a different leadership style, and some situations might need a different sort of approach to leadership. These models will guide you and help you see what is required depending on the situation at hand.

11.1
Communication

Communication is so important, because when you listen and take other people's opinions into consideration, you show respect, and you will gain a lot of respect in return. The simple expression that we have two ears and one mouth is so true in this regard. Within communication, listening is a very important part, especially if you want to be listened to as well.

To involve employees, give them the important insight that they are needed in the process, and it will motivate them at work. Employees that work hands-on have the information on what works and what doesn't work, so listen to them. If they complain, listen. It is not a bad thing that they get their disappointment out in words. That is better than having employees talking about it and slowing down the productivity because of disappointments.

Make notes of the input and suggestions from the employees. Make an overview. Again, do not make it too complex. If you train yourself to make these overviews, you will get the skill to overview things. But, don't miss out on important details. I will talk about this in the next chapter.

When you have trained your decision-making skills in private, you will get a lot of use out of this within your professional life. You have listened. You have mapped it out with input from others in the management team if you have one, or with some representatives from your coworkers. Make a plan, and present it either to the management team, if you have one, or to your coworkers. A detailed plan can be delegated if you have some outlines along the way. A clear vision, clear goals along the way, the words of conduct and the values within the company should be included in the plan.

Try not to do the whole plan yourself with every detail. Include people, but show the guidelines, the dos and don'ts, and what is expected. Here again it is very important to ask what the expected outcome is. What will happen if it is not reached? Do you have a plan A and a plan B? Try to discuss the different situations that might occur. When the plan is made in detail, decide on adjustments, explain why they have been chosen, and then execute the decision. Try to make the invested time from everyone as optimal as possible. You can really use communication skills to shorten the process of decision-making and to get people onboard and to accept the decisions needed.

There is no point waiting for people to get ready for a change before you make it. That is not professional from anyone's perspective. Explain the problem that is to be solved. Take into consideration different opinions and suggestions. Map out into a plan with different scenarios taken into consideration too. And involve the right people with diversity in the sense of experience within the company and other needed expertise. You will then be ready to make the decision.

11.2
Business Intelligence to Another Level

Business Intelligence (BI) is about adding more technical solutions and software where machines do the work for us. We are looking for statistics unaffected by human misunderstanding or modifications. You even get an email Friday afternoon with suggestions on how to improve next week within certain areas at work from a robot.

Stereotypes are not the truth of how a workplace of humans looks. You can try to handle everyone like a stereotype at work, and see how far that goes. That view of employees belongs to the early 1920s. The famous Hawthorne experiment showed that one hundred years ago. It has been used to show that people work better under supervision.

But the more modern interpretation is that production increases when people are seen, taken into consideration, and feel that there are leaders within the company that really care about them. The Human Resources movement has contributed to that development in the last half century.

Back one hundred years ago, it was engineers and psychologists who wanted to measure and find out what motivated people. Now we know, thanks to much study on this interesting field. And my field of study, a master's degree in business, is the result of this research. This is a younger field of study than engineering and psychology.

It is like turning the clock backwards one hundred years to before the famous Hawthorne experiment if we view Business Intelligence, BI, as something technical to replace everyday work life innovations. People with both new and longer experience often come up with solutions to problems using their experience or knowledge. This gives them the feeling of fulfilment and involvement needed to contribute and to make a difference. That is a motivation factor in itself.

Our fantastic intelligence as humans will take BI to another level if we really used the research that has been done in the last century. We don't have to reinvent the wheel, metaphorically speaking.

The solution is more diverse management teams, not only from the perspective of gender, but also from the perspective of work experience and educational background, as my model here explains. To interact with and take advantage of everyone's strengths are very smart moves within leadership.

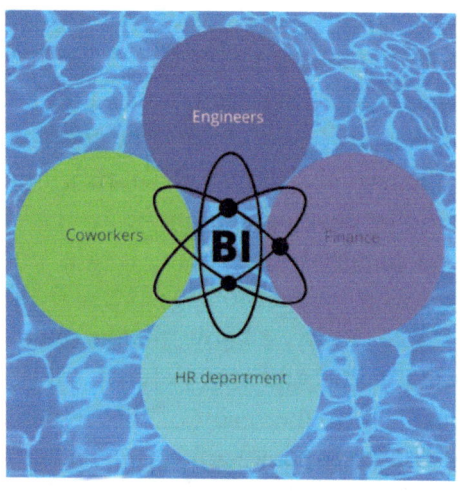

11.3
Leadership and You

Leadership starts with you and your ability to control and master your feelings and behaviors. You will feel more secure, and view situations from more than one perspective. You listen, and gather information. This helps you, together with past experiences, to decide if you need to do something.

Douglas McGregor has been called the creator of the Human Resources movement, and one of his famous models will be included in the next chapter. But his very simple model about making decisions I will take up here.

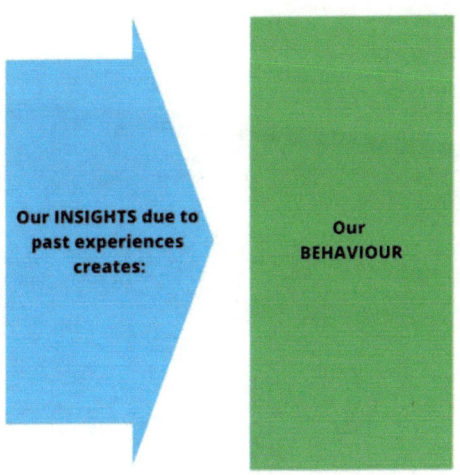

Douglas McGregor showed that our past insights and conclusions, drawn from past experiences, create our behavior. Think about this for a moment.

This is kind of basic, but the interesting thing is that when we deal with new situations in life, we still use our past experience and expect or hope that it will work again. That can create a terrible outcome if we either neglect possible outcomes because they have never occurred before, or if we haven't had to deal with this new situation.

We therefore need to stay openminded toward new possibilities and new outcomes as well as familiar situations, since circumstances might have changed a lot. This book is written during the outbreak of the COVID-19 pandemic, which has changed the market enormously and unexpectedly.

12
Structure Design

Making the lists mentioned earlier is a very useful tool and, when you have developed the speed to use them, they can be very efficient. Of course, where you save your documents and what folders you put them in is key. Map them into the different topics of importance to you, and separate private documents from business ones, of course.

If you write too much and don't sort them into topics, you will end up with loads of documents and no overview. Structure is made so that you can get a quick overview and ease your mind of unimportant things.

Sharing documents on a cloud service that everyone has access to at work or within the leadership team has so many advantages. One is that people are forced into a chosen structure regarding how to name documents and what they should contain. Have short weekly meetings to discuss how things are working and if any structure needs to be adjusted. It is important to try things and then evaluate them regularly to know if they are useful and have a good work flow. Employees will see that practical utility is of utmost importance, and they will feel that they are taken into consideration. The whole point is to save time, because administration is not intended to be inefficient and expensive nowadays.

Checklists are easily done in Excel or Numbers, but

make it easy and not time consuming. It should be easy to find and update the files. The same thing with a word document; the rule to only make a one pager to inform or to remember things of importance is very good. You don't want to be stuck in administration with too many documents that take time to read and to keep updated. Keep it as simple as possible, and structure how and when things are to be adjusted. It should be easy to find the information needed for one's job. It is a very good idea to keep templates where they are easy to find.

A common structure for administration is very smart. It avoids bureaucracy and old ways of handling administration. Everyone is forced into the new way of administration, the efficient way.

12.1
Details vs an Overview

An expert is good on details and can easily identify what is of importance within their field. No-one can be an expert on everything; usually you are an expert within one field of study, so choose your area of expertise. Details are important, but it is more important as a business leader to be a generalist in many different areas. You should have a solid overview of things both in your personal life and within your company.

It is a skill to learn how to sort out what is important to know from all the details. The problem is that many people believe that they have to be the expert in many areas at work and in life. And some even neglect to get the overview skills. They think that they can always ask someone else, but this is very time consuming both for you and others.

The main thing here is to learn to be a generalist in different areas. Avoid being stuck in decision-making because of bottleneck issues waiting for someone else. We have discussed decision-making in a previous chapter, but it is so important that I want to address it again. If you have a wide area of overview competence, then you can make a lot of decisions by yourself according to the company's policy.

Endless meetings with discussions because of lack of knowledge are really a waste of time. The whole idea of an internship is to get to know the company and how things work at the company. I do not just mean the products or the services. The culture is of course involved in decision-making processes within a company, and within a family too. Try to take away the prestige of decision-making, because it will take a lot of valuable time. Everybody's energy ought to be used on more important matters, like moving forward instead of being stuck in no-man's land.

Being focused too much on details can block you from growth. It is impossible to be an expert in many fields; usually you can be expert in a maximum of two areas. Learn how to become a generalist in other areas. You will feel less stressed and will learn so much more. The notion that you have to be an expert in everything is also something that affects your relationship with others negatively. Do you always have to win every argument or get the last word in a conversation to show that you know everything? No, no one does. Being too focused on details and the thought that you have to learn everything will block you. You will not have any energy left to explore other areas more generally.

You will also miss out on the joy of discussions with others in their areas of expertise. They will love to talk to you about it, and they can give you advice and short cuts if you just put your mind to it and listen.

12.2
Delegate and Excel Together

Here you will also be helped by having a good structure. You only need a checklist perhaps, to see what has been done and what must be done next. This depends on your company, of course, but don't use your energy in trying to know everything in detail. Trust other people within your company. If you have trouble with trust, build it; give people an assignment, and tell them kindly what result you expect and how to document it, according to your chosen structure.

People grow when you show trust and they grow by completing assignments. This way, they can contribute in their area of knowledge and try their wings, so to speak.

As we have said, no-one can be an expert on everything, just a few things. And no-one can have control over every detail that goes on within the company. So, delegate and the pressure on your shoulders will loosen its grip. Release each employee's energy and ability to grow within the company and you will feel the power of cooperation instead of competition within a company, or a family.

To delegate means that more can be done. A strong team with trust built on goals achieved in the past is almost unstoppable.

13
Uncertainty

During the COVID-19 pandemic much uncertainty was created, and many arguments about the right move against this uncertainty were made. Before COVID-19, we thought we had it all planned out. After COVID-19, we realized that we didn't. What I am saying is that there has always been a lot of uncertainty, but we expected things to happen as we had planned. Otherwise, it was bad planning.

People in general are worried and openly speak about uncertainty like never before. This new focus in life makes decision-making harder for people in general. Discovering the high risk of uncertainty makes customers slow down their decision-making or put it on hold. Our whole economy is built on the idea that the wheel of economy is constantly spinning. If market after market is put on hold, that is a very serious threat to the economy.

This raises new requirements on people in marketing, but also leaders in companies, to address uncertainty so that it doesn't stop business.

Uncertainty among employees is important to solve. Of course, as a leader you must solve your own uncertainty and cope with it. You can only do your best within your ability; beyond that, there is uncertainty. If you really take care of yourself, you will be strong enough both to cope with your own uncertainty and to encourage others.

A good thing to say is, "I am worried too." Show that you are a human being, not a machine. Talk to the employees and take it as a subject to discuss at coffee breaks and internal weekly meetings. It is important that everyone feels that they have a forum to talk about it. Otherwise, they will talk about it while they work and slow down the production even more. It will take different amounts of time for people to digest what is happening and try to cope with it. If you set an example and choose when and how to talk about it at work, everyone within the company will gain a lot. Everyone will feel safer and less worried.

To deal with uncertainty in the market requires personnel that can to some extent deal with their own uncertainty. Have short meetings at work with the employees at a time of your choice, and give them reasonable sentences that they can use when they interact with the customers. Schedule weekly meetings to create an atmosphere where you can discuss any suitable topic. This will save you a lot of time and energy. People will know that these meetings exist and will feel like they are really taken care of, that their worries matter, and that they are listened to.

Customers delaying their decision to buy can be a really tough situation to solve.

One thing to do is to really look over your internal routines and make it more efficient, especially with the administration. I have worked for decades within administration and have seen a lot of inefficiency in that area, even at large companies. Of course, if people are afraid of being laid off, they will hesitate to come up with ideas to simplify and make things quicker. You should therefore always be up for making your company more efficient, and reward such behaviors in the workplace. People will value contributing to change as rewarding, and not see it as a threat.

A smart organization is always moving forward and improving, and all the employees should be used to it. This is very important when uncertainty occurs, because you as a business leader will need all the cooperation you can get.

If the customer delays their decision to buy, more personnel might be needed in this area of the company. People who get transferred from other departments and are new to sales can come up with really good ideas.

People who are new to something often ask the question, "Why?" See if you can brainstorm some new tactics to approach this new situation with the customers.

Of course, it can be challenging to switch from administration to sales, but it's a good idea to really give it a try instead of being laid off and unemployed.

A successful team uses each member's strengths and viewpoint in new or challenging situations. Being swift to adapt to new circumstances will most likely be the focus of the market for the upcoming year.

14
Dealing with Crisis

Dealing with crisis is even more challenging than dealing with uncertainty. I worked at a bank office in a small town temporarily, while I studied for my master's degree in business. I had just finished my last week and left for some time off with my family before the school started again for the autumn. A few weeks later, the bank was robbed. Two employees were threatened with a gun, but no-one got injured. This all happened very quickly. The disguised man ran away with some money and left in his car. This was a small town in the countryside where nothing had ever happened.

No one was injured, but the shock stayed. The employees never got back to work again from anxiety, the picture of the robbery repeating in their minds. Employees within banks and other places where there is cash need to be trained on how to deal with this. These employees were, and thanks to that no-one was injured. But could more have been done to prepare for the scenario? This is an interesting question.

Within the bank, they discussed the statement, "The opportunity makes a thief." From that reasoning, many risk analysis were made to try to identify and take away any opportunities for theft to occur. Risk analysis within any company is very important to try to foresee and prevent accidents and possible external threats. This trains both people and the company to be more careful as well, to take responsibility for products and the people involved both inside and outside the company.

When a crisis happens, people need to talk about it to digest what has happened. Our body reacts with shock and we need a lot of rest; it is our body's way to say that now we need to go down on kind of a slow-motion mode. Rest and the ability to talk to people who really listen and care are very important. A crisis is a stressful situation, and what works for dealing with a situation of high pressure and stress is applicable when dealing with crisis. We need to talk about it a lot, go through every detail, and let the emotions take care of our reactions.

Abraham Maslow's Theory of Motivation is also called the hierarchy of needs.

In this theory, we have the basic needs that we all need as humans. If any of these basic needs of security, and food, water, shelter, love and understanding are missing in our life we are at risk of not taking care of ourselves. Being loved and respected is so important for self-love. It makes us feel that life truly matters and that we are appreciated for who we are.

A healthy organization within a company understands that we have these important basic needs as humans. We call it Human Resources, HR, for this reason.

15
Building Business Confidence

It all starts with you. You will take how you deal with personal matters with you to your job. We all have bad days, but don't use it as an excuse to be in a bad mood and to spread bad vibes. Learn how to cope with life.

Crises and other challenging events are a part of life. This is not a way to minimize tragic things that happen, not at all. It is more a way to not become paralyzed for a long time because of things that do happen. When you go through life and bad things do happen to you, try to find things that can help you learn to become stronger. This can be like fuel for you on your way to achieve your goals, it can become your "Why," as many within personal development call it. Your "Why" is the reason you do things, your source of energy you carry. It helps you to not give up on your goals and dreams. Your "Why" will help you to take down the dreams from the clouds. I love that statement.

Difficult times can make you strong, because you have been around and know a thing and two. It is very important to view your experience in life as an asset you are supposed to put into practice to do good things. Bad things can be used as a "no go option."

We can ride out storms and sad things worse than we ever imagined. We have it built into ourselves. But often, we scare ourselves, so we hesitate or come to the conclusion that it is over for us because of either a failure or a tragedy that we have fallen victim to. But try to use this as an experience that you can cope with. One day at a time is a very important way to start with tragic events. At least you are trying, and your subconscious will reward yourself with confidence and self-love. You will also show yourself that you can and will be strong again.

Good habits strengthen us, both subconsciously and consciously. Bad habits do too. It's a choice; add one good habit each day if you are just starting out and see the energy you will gain to continue. Bad habits destroy our life one day at a time. Good habits prolong our life, and it will be a healthier life too. Take care of yourself. You need that. It starts with you taking yourself places.

Stepping into work with this attitude will certainly make a huge difference with your career. Associate with people that build you up, and do the same for them. That is how successful teams are built. A successful team that really use everyone's skills is unstoppable. And you are unstoppable on your way to achieve your goals if you use good habits in your everyday life. I wish you the very best for you on your path to achieving good things in life for yourself and others.